Hillary Clinton
힐러리 클린턴

Biography Comic
who? ④ Hillary Clinton

개정판 1쇄 인쇄 2014년 3월 5일
개정판 1쇄 발행 2014년 3월 10일

글 안형모
그림 스튜디오 청비
번역 자넷 재완 신
감수 김수희
펴낸이 김선식

책임편집 김선영 **디자인** 박효영
콘텐츠개발팀장 김선영 **콘텐츠개발팀** 박효영, 이유미, 김선민, 조서인
마케팅본부 이상혁

펴낸곳 스튜디오 다산 **출판등록** 2013년 11월 1일 제414-81-37694
주소 경기도 파주시 회동길 37-14 3층
전화 02-702-1724(기획편집) 02-703-1725(마케팅) 02-704-1724(경영관리)
팩스 02-703-2219 **who클럽** cafe.naver.com/dasankids
종이 월드페이퍼(주) | **인쇄** (주)현문 | **제본** 광성문화사

ISBN 979-11-5639-026-8 (14740)

who?
Hillary
Clinton
힐러리 클린턴

글 안형모 | 그림 **스튜디오 청비** | 번역 **자넷 재완 신** | 감수 **김수희**

Dasan Kid

Hillary Clinton

American Politician, October 26, 1947~ present

Hillary Rodham was born on October 26, 1947 in Chicago, Illinois. Her father, Hugh Rodham, owned a small textiles business and was an ardent Republican who raised his children strictly. Her mother, Dorothy Rodham, was a housewife who inspired her to have courage and strength in all circumstances.

Besides her parents, Rodham had two teachers who had a great influence on her: her history teacher, Paul Carlson, and Pastor Don Jones, who led a church program called the University of Life. It was under diverse influences such as these that Hillary Rodham began to develop her political identity.

During her years of studies at Wellesley, Rodham achieved outstanding grades and was politically active on campus. After graduating, Rodham went to Yale Law School where she met her future husband, Bill Clinton, who was then aspiring to become a politician.

Bill Clinton eventually became elected Governor of Arkansas and entered the world of politics. At the same time, Hillary started working for Rose Law Firm and represented the poor and underprivileged. Later she was made chair of several committees on children and education in Arkansas, and was successful in implementing some bold reforms and improving the education system among the rural poor.

She was appointed Chair of the National Health Care Reform Committee and demonstrated her outstanding political prowess in health care and education issues. After eight years in the White House, she was elected U.S. Senator of New York and continued to demonstrate her strong political skills. Finally, she strived to become the first female president of the United States and ran to become the Democratic presidential candidate.

Unfortunately, she lost the race to Barack Obama, who became the first African-American president. Obama however, recognized her ability and appointed her to be Secretary of State. Hillary Clinton is now a world-renowned female leader, known for her intelligence, confidence, and will to succeed.

힐러리 클린턴

미국의 정치가, 1947년 10월 26일~

힐러리는 1947년 10월 26일, 미국 일리노이 주 시카고에서 태어났습니다. 작은 직물 회사를 운영하던 아버지 휴 로댐은 열렬한 공화당 지지자로 엄격한 교육을 하였고 평범한 가정주부였던 어머니 도로시 로댐은 힐러리가 용기를 가지고 언제나 당당할 수 있도록 힘을 불어넣어 주었습니다.

힐러리에게는 부모님 외에 큰 영향을 주었던 두 명의 스승이 있었습니다. 한 사람은 학교에서 역사를 가르치던 폴 칼슨 선생님이고, 다른 한 사람은 교회에서 인생대학을 운영하던 돈 존스 목사님이었습니다. 힐러리는 이런 다양한 환경 속에서 자신의 정체성을 키우며 성장해 갔습니다.

대학 재학 시절에 우수한 학업 성적과 활발한 정치 활동으로 주목을 받던 힐러리는 이후 예일 대학교 법학대학원에 진학하여 정치인을 꿈꾸던 빌 클린턴을 만나고, 졸업 후 결혼을 하게 됩니다.

빌 클린턴은 아칸소 주 주지사에 당선되어 정치에 입문하고, 힐러리는 로즈 법률 사무소에서 변호사로 일하며 약자의 편에 서기 위해 노력했습니다. 아칸소 주의 아동과 교육에 관한 문제를 담당하게 되면서 과감한 개혁을 실천하여 능력을 인정받기도 했습니다.

힐러리는 영부인이 된 후에도 '미국보건관리개혁 대책위원회'의 의장직을 맡아 교육, 의료 분야에서 뛰어난 능력을 발휘했습니다. 이후 뉴욕 주 상원 의원에 당선되어 정치인으로서의 탁월한 능력을 입증하면서 마침내 미국 최초의 여성 대통령이 되기 위해 민주당 경선에 출마하기에 이릅니다.

아쉽게도 대통령 도전에는 실패하지만 미국 최초의 흑인 대통령 오바마에 의해 능력을 높이 평가받아 국무장관에 임명되었고 현재 세계적인 여성 리더로서 큰 활약을 하고 있습니다.

이 책을 만든 사람들

글 · 안형모

어린이들의 꿈을 키워 주는 재미있고 유익한 만화를 만들기 위해 즐겁게 작업하고 있습니다. 인물 이야기를 통해 위인들의 성공적인 업적보다는 성공에 이르기까지 과정과 노력을 담기 위해 노력합니다. 『천추태후』, 『통째로 한국사 1, 2』, 『호동왕자와 낭랑공주』 등의 만화 시나리오를 썼습니다.

그림 · 스튜디오 청비

기발한 상상력을 바탕으로 새롭고 재미있는 콘텐츠를 만들어 내는 만화 창작 집단입니다. 어린이들이 책을 읽고 큰 꿈을 품기를 바라는 마음으로 즐겁게 작업하고 있습니다. 작품으로 『성철 스님』, 『아 다르고 어 다른 우리말 101가지』, 『반기문 유엔 사무총장의 꿈과 도전』 등이 있습니다.

번역 · 자넷 재완 신(Janet Jaywan Shin)

미국 메릴랜드 주에서 태어나고 자랐습니다. 메릴랜드 대학교에서 언어학을 전공하고 UCLA에서 응용언어학 석사 학위를 취득했습니다. 서울대학교 언어교육원에서 전임 강사, 서울대학교 사범대학교 영어교육과에서 초빙교수로 일했습니다. 감수한 책으로 『서울대생한테 비밀 영어과외받기』가 있고 고등학교 영어 교과서 교정 작업에 참여했습니다.

감수 · 김수희

연세대학교에서 역사를 전공했습니다. 이후 한국뿐 아니라 일본, 미국에서 한국어, 일본어, 영어를 가르쳐 왔으며 부모를 위한 영어교육용 책을 썼습니다. 영어교육채널 EBSe '엄마표 영어특강'에서 강의를 하며 홈스쿨, 알파벳과 파닉스, 다차원 테마 영어 수업 기법을 알리고 있습니다. 전국 각지에서 어린이 영어 교육에 대한 강연을 하며 창의적이고 열정적인 교수법으로 영어를 배우고자 하는 어린이와 부모들에게 많은 도움을 주고 있습니다.

Hillary Clinton

When Hillary Clinton was young, instead of a politician, what did she want to be when she grew up?

a. Teacher
b. Astronaut
c. Scientist

Answer: b

Contents

01 How to Face Your Fears

Track 01 ▶

Park Ridge, Illinois. 1950.

This is where we'll be living from now on.

Wow! This is awesome!

With the energy you're using to chatter, why don't you move some boxes?

Alright, honey.

I'll help too!

11

So you're saying it's our fault?

Suzy! Someone's coming!

You're lucky this time.

The pot's all broken!

Hillary! Did you do this?

Sorry, Daddy.

You're not concentrating on what you're doing. You'd better not break anything else!

14

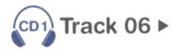

Five years later,

Today I want you to write the numbers 1 to 1000 in your notebook.

That's gonna take forever!

That's too hard!

Even though it seems hard, write each one carefully, one by one.

Yes, ma'am.

I can't do anymore.

I give up too.

20

What's Dad going to say if you buy a new outfit and stop wearing your perfectly fine clothes? You're just going to get yelled at for asking.

I knew you'd say that...

Mom's always afraid of what Dad's gonna say.

What?

Huh? They lost.

Tsk, tsk. Two outs with the bases loaded, but they couldn't make a single run.

Doin' good. Hit one out of the park.

That makes me mad. With just one more hit, the Chicago Cubs could've won.

Yuck! I hate the news!

Enough of baseball. Let's watch the news.

A congressman has been detained under the suspicion of accepting bribes.

NEWS NEV

Those are the worst kind of people. When I see crooked businessmen or corrupt politicians, I get so mad.

I hate them too.

What do you know?

The only party that can lead this nation right is the Republican party.

That's right.

That's why I like the Republican party too.

Don't try to know about grownups' business. Go to your room and study.

But I finished all my homework. Should I do tomorrow's homework?

24

If we can't find anything at all, we could always go and work for Dad.

Sigh.

Hey, it's snowing!

Wow! It's snowing!

Hillary, I'm cold.

I'll find the toothpaste. Why don't you two go in?

Aha, there it is!

I found it, Hillary! Hehe.

29

Don't worry, Mom…

The next day...

I'm going to go to school now.

Do you have a Girl Scout meeting today?

No. I just felt like wearing my uniform.

It's really comfortable. I should've worn it more all along!

Ok. Have a good day at school.

Mom…

Yeah? What is it?

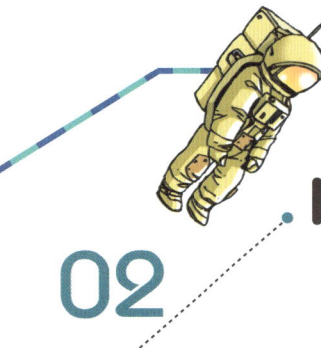

02 I Want to Be an Astronaut

 **Track 12 ▶**

Hillary, can I borrow some money? Dad's not giving us any allowance.

I don't have much either.

Here!

Thanks!

Sir, do you have any job openings here?

For you?

How old are you?

Thirteen.

You're kinda young. You think you can do it?

Whatever you give me, I'll do it! Please!

You'd be helping clean up the park. Wanna give it a try?

Yes, sir!

Hillary began to earn her own spending money working at a small park in Park Ridge.

Do you think you can do it?

Well…

Yes, ma'am. I'll give it a try.

Hillary was selected to be the safety patrol captain of her school. Her job was to help mitigate fights and conflicts among students.

Stop it!

What's wrong? We just wanna get to know you better. Ha ha ha!

Hey! Stop! Hillary's coming!

What? Hillary? Run!

I'm a student from Park Ridge, Illinois. And I would like to apply to become an astronaut.

There. I can't wait for the reply.

When Louis XIV said, "I am the state."

he was talking about absolute power.

Hillary! Is there something you'd like to tell all of us?

Yes. I applied to NASA to become an astronaut.

Are you serious?

Wow! That's great.

You're really going to become an astronaut?

And be on TV?

Hmmm.

Well, it hasn't happened yet.

Hillary, I really hope you get to be an astronaut.

Yeah, I'm excited about it too. I wish the reply comes soon.

A few days later...

I'm dying to see what they wrote.

Hillary! You got a letter from NASA.

Really?

Dear Miss Hillary Rodham,
We are sorry,
but we cannot recruit
women to become astronauts.

What?

Hillary was shocked to find out that she was rejected based on the fact that she was a girl.

How can this be? Because I'm a girl?

Women can't become astronauts? That's ridiculous!

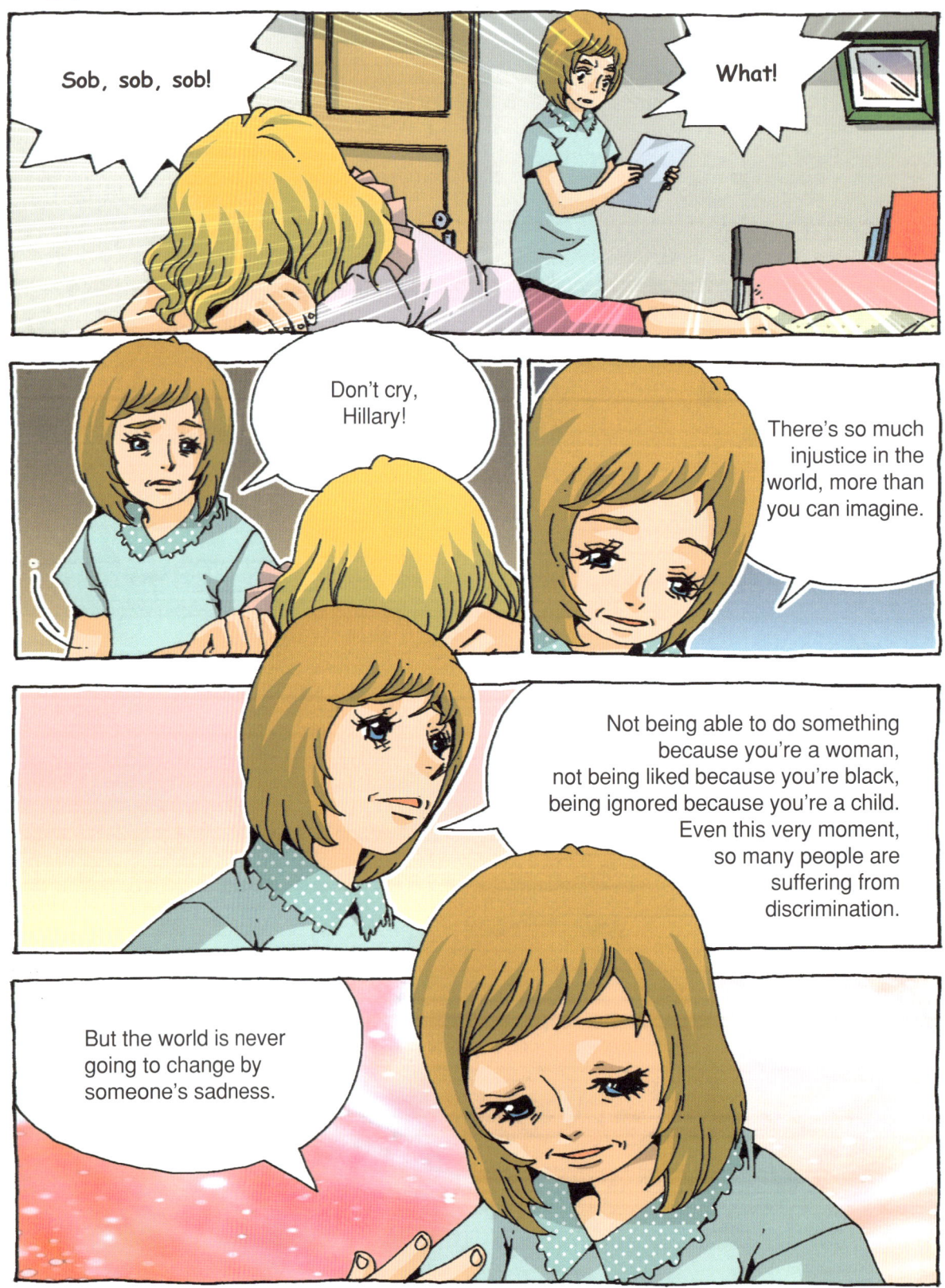

46

47

Ding dong~

Ding dong~

Betsy, do you know anything about Pastor Donald Jones?

I heard he served in the Navy, then went to seminary, and has just graduated.

I guess we'll learn more about him at the University of Life.

Oh! It's already started.

We can not just sit around if we want to get rid of these kinds of discrimination.

Only when we put our faith into action can we break down the walls of discrimination.

We can see it in the black civil rights movement that's happening in the South.

Faith into action?

That's right.
If discrimination
exists, then we
have to fight it.

I'm going to fight
and change
this world that
discriminates
against girls.

I'll show them that
there's nothing
women can't do.

This Pastor Jones is
a very progressive thinker.
Hillary should not be influenced
by someone like him.

03 The World Outside of Park Ridge

I'm always looking forward to Thursdays and the weekend when we get to go to the University of Life.

You know we're going to go visit a black church in Chicago today.

The reason we're visiting a black church is because I want you to know more about the world outside of Park Ridge.

You're going to get a better idea about racial discrimination when you talk to blacks or Hispanics.

Alright, let's go!

Yeah!

At a black church in Chicago

Alright, now let's start the discussion.

Nice to meet you.

Yeah.

I'd like to hear what you all think about the Freedom Ride movement going on in the South.

What's that?

I don't know either.

Umm...

The Freedom Ride movement is trying to abolish racial discrimination on trains operating in and across states.

It's trying to correct the unjust treatment blacks have been experiencing until now.

Wow!

Right on! What do you think about this movement?

I support it. This kind of baseless discrimination has to be done away with.

Wow!

It gives me hope to hear that kind of thinking from a white girl!

I've been hurt by discrimination too. That's cool that they're encouraged by me.

She's very mature for her age.

Come back again some time.
Sure!
What did you think?
It was great. I hope we can do this more often.
Let's do that.
This place...
I came here once with my dad when I was little.
He brought us here and compared our lives with these starving kids'.
Look at these kids.
Now can you see how well we're living?
Oh, dear!

57

You have some strong memories of this place.

It's sad that these kids here are still starving just like the kids I saw back then.

Do you want this?

Thank you!

Things are going to get better.
Don't lose hope, okay?

Will that day really come?

Yeah.

I always wanted to be a track star and be in the Olympics…

58

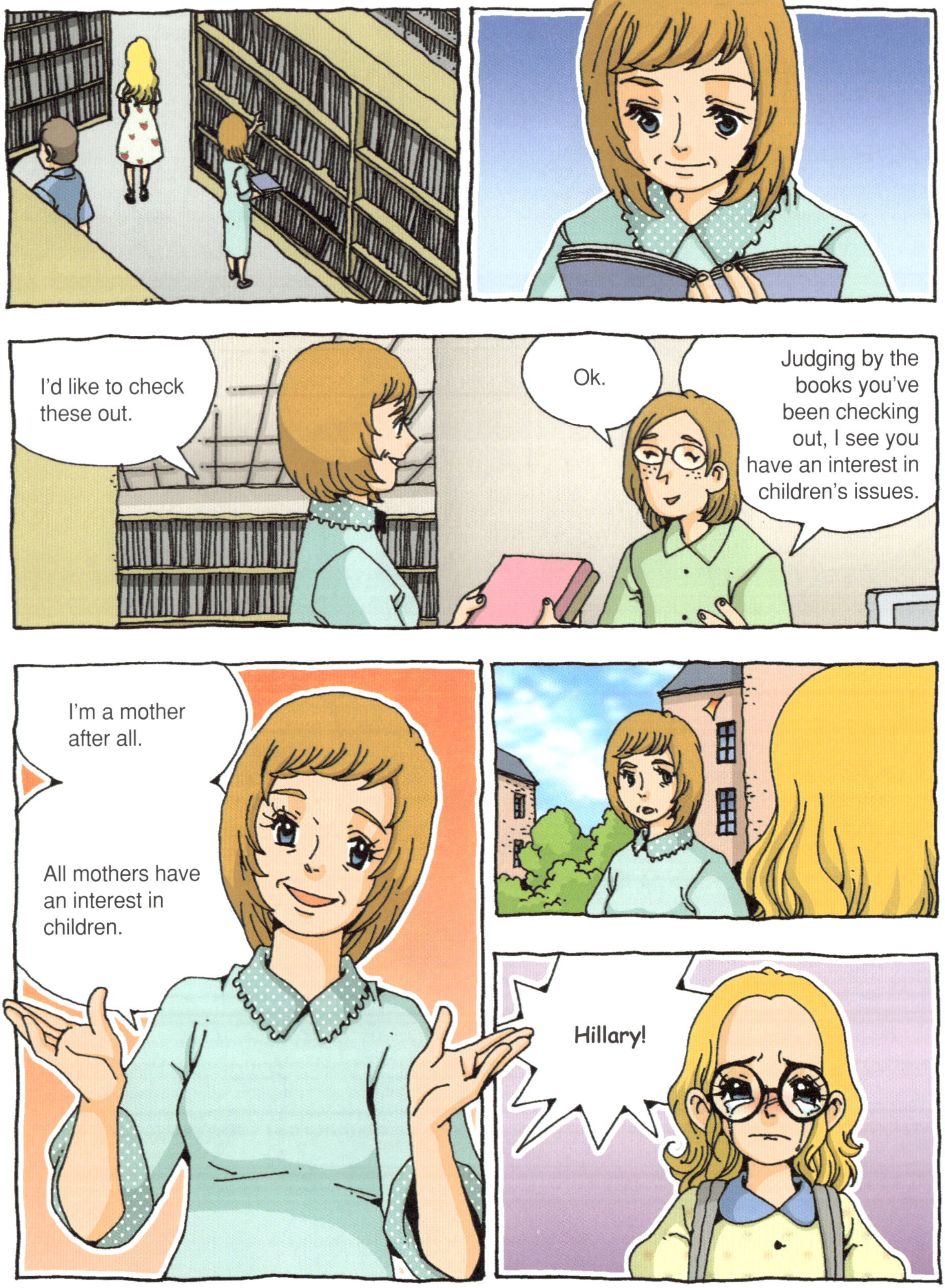

I'd like to check these out.

Ok.

Judging by the books you've been checking out, I see you have an interest in children's issues.

I'm a mother after all.

All mothers have an interest in children.

Hillary!

When I was living with my grandmother, if I didn't obey her, she'd lock me up in a room or beat me. Unlike other kids, I didn't grow up with much love.

My brother and I ended up running away and I had to work as a house maid.

But I didn't give up hope and that hope still keeps me going today.

And that hope has given me a precious family!

Don't worry. Those kids have a chance too.

Ok, mom.

What if we hold a mini-Olympics for the kids?

Really? Mini Olympics?

Yeah. While the events are going on, we can raise money by selling cookies to the spectators.

That's a good idea.

Ok! I'm in!

65

Isn't she the girl we talked to in Chicago?

Yup.

She's gonna compete in today's race.

What?

But your legs are…

It's ok. I can still run.

Imagine you're in the Olympics and run with all you've got.

Alright!

Runners, please line up at the starting line.

It's your turn.

66

When I grow up, I want to help children who are in difficult circumstances.

That's great.

Hillary was able to experience many things through Pastor Donald Jones' University of Life.

She was able to expand her cultural knowledge by going to art exhibits and discussing classical literature.

She was even able to have a few words with Martin Luther King, Jr., after listening to his speech.

Amen

The purpose of life is not just the pursuit of happiness. The true purpose of life is to follow the purpose God has given to you.

Thank you for your speech. It was quite moving.

Thank you for your interest in what I had to say.

If we can gather each person's interest and efforts together, there will be a big change in society.

The University of Life served to broaden Hillary's world beyond Park Ridge.

Wow, I don't think I can ever forget Reverend King's speech today.

Me neither.

Is this you?

Is this really you in the newspaper?

Yeah.

In the end, both Paul Carlson, the students' teacher at school, and the person he opposed, Pastor Donald Jones, left after two years at the church.

04 Yet Another Setback

CD1 Track 33 ▶

Hillary!

Hi, Mr. Carlson.

It's too bad what happened to Pastor Jones. He was trying to teach you all some strange ideas.

We couldn't ignore it any longer.

I understand.

I'm glad. Thank you.

Yikes. To think that guys who think like that almost became our school president.

Betsy, I'm thinking of running for student body president, too.

You are?

Are you serious? There's never been a girl president before.

That's exactly why I want to do it.

I'm going to show them that girls can be not only supporters but presidents.

Yes, b-but...

 Track 36 ▶

You know about the candidate speech rally tomorrow, don't you?

Speech rally?

Yeah! It's a great chance to win more votes. You've really gotta do well.

But I've never given a speech in my life.

Really?

If you don't think you can do it, would you rather just quit now? It's not easy to give a speech in front of 5,000 people.

No way! I can't quit!

I'm going to just do it! I must.

Well, okay...

80

Standing in front of a lot of people makes me soooo nervous.

Are you sure you can do it?

If I can't give my speech today because I'm scared, I won't ever be able to do anything.

Yeah.
I can do it.

Fellow classmates!
There exists
a division among us.

Everyone seemed to like her speech.

She might actually win the election.

Don't worry. That's not going to happen.

We'll show them once and for all that girls becoming school president is nothing but a figment of their imagination.

You were great, Hillary! I didn't know you could give such a great speech.

Thanks, Betsy!

I could do it because I didn't give up. Just like the way my mom taught me when I was little, to overcome my fears.

Hey, it's Hillary.

She's got the highest percentage of supporters so far. She just might become president.

Hi, Mr. Carlson!

Hi there, Hillary. You must be pretty busy with all the campaigning.

Don't push yourself too hard. Whatever the outcome, consider it a good experience.

A good experience?

Excuse me?

You know how people feel these days. It's still hard for many to accept a female as a leader.

Hillary has really bad eyes. If she doesn't wear her glasses, she can't even recognize the person standing in front of her.

What's gonna happen if she messes something up while she's president because of her bad eyes?

Ha ha ha ha!

That's not all. She tries really hard to look good to the teachers. But to us, she's known to be as cold as ice.

Isn't that why her nickname is Frigid Nun?

I didn't know that about her. How disappointing.

Liar! How can he make such groundless personal attacks?

Hillary, let's not just stand around. Let's make our own personal attacks.

I don't want to do that.

Not every student will fall for those lies.

Let's just concentrate on what we have to do, Betsy.

B-, But.

If you vote for me, I'll work hard to create a good academic atmosphere for our school!

The other candidates began a negative campaign personally attacking Hillary.

In the end,
Hillary lost the election.

We lost, Hillary.

See, we should've attacked our opponents more.

You were right, Betsy!

Next time, I'm not going to just let myself be attacked. Next time!

The results of the election must not have been good.

The bigger your dreams the better!

You're right, Mom! Hehe!

Have you thought about which college you want to go to?

Yeah, I want to go to Wellesley College, the well-known women's college on the East Coast.

That far away?

You want me to be the first female Supreme Court justice, don't you?

That's right.

I need to go to a school like Wellesley to fulfill that dream, to fulfill my life.

Please trust me and let me go.

Hillary…

92

05   Blooming at Wellesley College

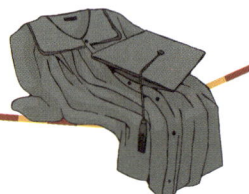

 Track 01 ▶

In the fall of 1965, Hillary Rodham entered Wellesley College. While Rodham was in college in the 1960s, it was an era of confusion and change with the black civil rights movement and the Vietnam War raging.

The social atmosphere of that time had a big influence on Rodham's values.

I'm sending you there because the school regulations are strict. I will not put up with you straying from the rules in the least bit.

It took so much hard work to get into Wellesley.

To think that the goal of this school is to make a good housewife.

This was the first time Rodham was so far from home and living on her own. About a month into her first year at school, she felt lonely and confused.

This is so hard.

As she got used to college life, she regained the confidence she had before.

I'm going to fight to get our rights back from this backwards institution, our rights that have been trampled on.

As time passed, Rodham gradually began to do something about what she believed in.

We've got to start by getting rid of these ridiculous school regulations.

I heard they're having a meeting here to protest the core curriculum requirement.

That's right! You're in the right place.

But is this everyone?

We don't have enough people.

I must have gotten ahead of myself. There's hardly anyone here who wants toparticipate.

There's nothing to see. Let's just go.

Th-, The reason why there are only a few people here today is, that

most of the students are staying up all night at the library to do homework for these worthless required classes.

We're not at Wellesley to become good housewives. We're here to become contributing members of society.

We must get rid of these old school regulations that are holding us back!

ClapClapClap

Down with the required core curriculum, right now!

Right now! Right now!

Impressive.

Did you say your name was Hillary? That was really impressive.

Do we know each other?

I'm the leader of the Young Republicans club on campus.

I heard you were a Republican party supporter. You wanna become a member of our group?

If it's Republican, I'm there.

Rodham joined the Young Republicans during her freshman year.

Everyone wants you to be the next president of our club.

C'mon, Hillary.

But I just joined. How can I be president?

That's not important.

An organization needs to have the most capable and energetic person to lead it.

After becoming the new president of the Young Republicans, Rodham and the other members did a lot to help campaign for the Republican presidential candidate.

You can do it, right?

Ok, I'll give it a try.

When the Attorney General of Massachusetts, Edward Brooke, ran for Senate, Rodham helped run a positive election campaign which contributed to his victory.

Congratulations, Senator!

Thanks to you all!

Rodham was active in many different campus groups and played an important role in each of them.

During her sophomore year, Rodham was class representative in the student government.

You can't tell by just looking at her, but she's a pretty amazing leader.

I want to be like her.

During her junior year at Wellesley, Rodham ran for college government president.

You should be student government president and talk with the administration to listen to our demands.

Hillary, there are a lot of people supporting you!

Student government president?

Hillary's a Republican. She holds the same views on the civil rights movement and the Vietnam War as the Republican party.

She doesn't want reform in our school or our society!

Now is the period of progressive change. Someone as conservative in her views as Hillary should not be student representative.

Unfair personal attacks!

I put up with it in high school because I didn't know any better, but I'm not going to put up with it this time.

Going door-to-door in the dorms, Rodham made efforts to clearly inform people about her views.

I'm not just blindly following the Republican party. I also support Democrat Eugene McCarthy's anti-war views.

I see.

We believe in you, Hillary!

I'm going to get rid of the outdated regulations. Vote for me.

Ok.

Hillary, how's the election campaign going?

Hey, Eldie!

After I heard you support Democrat Eugene McCarthy, I decided to vote for you.

Yeah, I don't agree with the Republican stance on the civil rights movement or the Vietnam War.

I don't know how someone as bright as you can be a Republican.

Who's that?

We took a political science class together in our freshman year.

She's former Secretary of State Dean Acheson's granddaughter.

That's why she's against the Republican party.

Our goal in life cannot be to merely become a good housewife.

We must become people who contribute to the development and growth of our society and country with our abilities.

Vote for Hillary!

Yeah!

It's finally election day tomorrow.

Yeah.

We've done our best, so now we just have to wait for the results.

The intense battle had ended and Rodham, with the support of many students, won the election for student government president.

You did it! Congratulations, Hillary!

I-, I can't believe it.

Professor, I just got elected president of our student government!

Can you believe it? How did this happen?

It happens every year. What's hard to believe about it? Ha ha ha!

Rodham worked hard as student government president.

Then one day, she received shocking news.

BAM

I can't believe it!

Why do these things keep happening!

Rodham participated in a large-scale demonstration of protest and grieving held at the city square.

And she also organized a demonstration on campus.

Abolish the restriction on black student admission!

Abolish it! Abolish it!

What is it exactly that you're asking for?

Having a quota on the number of black students is pure discrimination. We want to abolish the restriction on admission for black students.

Rodham contributed greatly in changing the school admissions policy to increase the quota of black students.

We will examine this issue thoroughly.

Thinking deeply about the civil rights movement and the Vietnam War, Rodham's political position gradually began to shift towards the Democratic party.

Students want to do away with the required curriculum and...

I have another request.

we feel it is necessary to get rid of the rules in which the school assumes the role of our parents.

Are you trying to change all of Wellesley's traditions?

Wellesley students are not children. Please treat us as adults.

Well, I never!...

During Rodham's term as president, the required curriculum as well as outdated regulations were, for the most part, done away with.

Down with the old regulations!

113

So now you support Democrat Eugene McCarthy and oppose everything that's Republican policy?

Expanding the war efforts is definitely a wrong move.

Even this very moment, hundreds of young people are dying on the battlegrounds.

When we were young, we fought for this country too.

Because of the noble sacrifice that took place, you can live comfortably today.

But is it true patriotism to go into a war that's avoidable, at the cost of many lives?

You talk just like a Democrat. Get out of my house!

You are not going to take no for an answer, I see.

That's right.

And who would be the student speaker?

Hillary Rodham, ma'am!

Me?

We all decided. You've got to listen to us this time.

Alright. If it's going to Hillary, then I will allow it.

Dean!

Actually, I --uh, umm.

I'm gonna be the student representative to give the graduation speech!

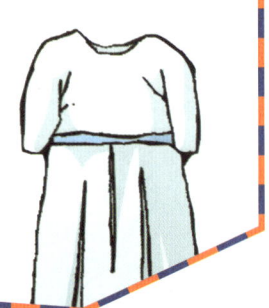

06 A Warm Heart

 **Track 16** ▶

In the fall of 1969, Hillary Rodham went to Yale Law School. Yale students were active in social issues like civil rights, anti-war sentiments, and women's rights.

The Vietnam War looks like it's going to expand into Cambodia.

We have to participate in the anti-war movement too.

Hillary, you're going to the demonstration too, aren't you?

But I'm against demonstrations using violence.

Gandhi and Reverend King's nonviolent resistance movements drew many people's sympathy and support.

Yeah.

124

You're right. But everyone's anger has reached its peak. I don't know if we can keep it from getting violent.

Let's try, anyway.

The government must stop oppressing the Black Panthers!

Stop the oppression!

End the Vietnam War!

End the war!

End the war!

127

League of Women Voters convention

Hi, I'm Hillary Rodham.

Yes, I heard about you from my husband.

He said you wanted to talk to me.

I heard you are starting an anti-poverty organization in Washington.

Could I work with you during my vacation?

Really?

You can work with me, but I don't have the funds to pay you.

That's ok. Just put me to work.

I want to work there, but my tuition is going to be an issue.

Later, Rodham received a grant from the Law Student Civil Rights Research Council, which enabled her to work with Edelman.

Please find out about the education and health of migrant workers' children.

Yes, Ma'am.

That's mine. Give it to me!

I hate you! Waaah!

Kids, let's not fight.

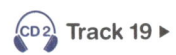

Sniff... snif...

Why are you crying?

I can't take part in *Holy Communion.

Why?

I need a white dress to take part in Communion. But my parents said they don't have money to buy me one.

Oh!

How sad! She doesn't have money to buy clothes.

What should I do? I barely have enough for myself with the funding from the Research Council.

*Holy Communion: a Catholic ritual to commemorate Christ's Last Supper.

Mom, there's this girl who can't partake in Communion because she doesn't have a white dress.

She can't partake in Communion because she doesn't have a white dress? What a shame...

You came all the way here, even though your body's still weak.

I'm a lot better. Don't worry.

I couldn't sleep thinking about that poor girl you were telling me about.

Oh, Mom! I shouldn't have said anything.

We'll take that white dress over there.

Yes, Ma'am.

133

But…

Thank you so much!

My dear Maria! Such kind people…

While doing this research, Rodham developed a strong concern for poverty-stricken children.

Let's go now.

Ok, Mom.

134

If you're going to keep looking at me, I'm going to look right back at you.

Wha-, What?

You've been staring at me.

Who's that?

That's Hillary Rodham. She gave a speech at her college graduation and was even featured in a magazine.

You seem pretty interested in her, Bill.

What? Me?

Hillary and Bill met again the following spring and soon began to like each other.

07 Devotion to Hope

CD2 Track 23 ▶

After completing their studies, Hillary Rodham and Bill Clinton went their own separate ways. Bill went to Arkansas to pursue politics. Rodham went to work as a lawyer for Edelman's newly established Children's Defense Fund.

Ms. Rodham, there's a phone call for you.

This is John Doar. I'm the head of the presidential impeachment investigation team.

Rodham got an unexpected opportunity to serve on the impeachment investigation team.

We're looking for five energetic lawyers to help with the impeachment investigation of President Richard Nixon.

Presidential impeachment?

!

This is a chance to witness history in the making.

Would you be interested?

Yes.

Finish up your work on the impeachment investigation and come to Arkansas. I think the University of Arkansas wants you to teach there.

Teach?

Rodham had to do an enormous amount of intense law research while doing the impeachment investigation.

Look into past U.S. impeachment cases and see if there are any precedents that we can refer to.

Yes, sir.

There were days when she worked for 18 hours straight but Rodham was able to faithfully do what was required.

President Nixon, however, resigned before getting impeached. As a result, the investigation came to an end.

Thank you everyone for your hard work. We got a lot done because of all your labor.

Now what are you going to do, Hillary?

I agreed to teach criminal law at the University of Arkansas.

Several years later, Bill Clinton proposes to Hillary Rodham, and the two are finally engaged to be married.

I bought this house for you. So, will you marry me? I can't live here by myself.

We sincerely pray that God would bless the future path of these two people.

You're not going to change your name to Clinton, even though you two are married?

No, I'm not.

Please try to understand.

That is ridiculous! Tradition says that a married woman uses the name of her husband.

I don't think that one is absolutely obliged to follow that.

What are you going to do if your decision affects your husband's career?

If something like that happens, know that you are responsible for it!

After getting married,
Hillary and Bill each did
their share of the housework.
They also gave each other space
to pursue different interests.

Bill Clinton worked hard
and finally became elected
as the Attorney General of
Arkansas.

Then two years later,
at the age of 32,
he became the governor
of Arkansas.

In 1980,
the Clintons' daughter,
Chelsea, was born.

We
love you,
sweetie!

I'm proud of
you, honey!

Then suddenly, in the midst of all these celebratory events, an unexpected misfortune occurred.

No!

Honey, I lost the re-election.

Bill Clinton lost the election for his second term as governor and was devastated.

Why doesn't the governor's wife use his last name?

She doesn't pay much attention to her appearance or even go to social events.

Tsk tsk! She must not know how much Arkansans hate that kind of thing.

How dare they!

Honey, I'm home.

Hey there.

Honey!

Plop

His failure feels like my own failure.

A lot of people were saying that because I didn't change my last name to Clinton, it hindered your chances of getting reelected.

Do you want me to change my name?

That's not true. A person's name is not for someone else to decide.

In 1982, Bill Clinton announced his running for governor once more. This time, Hillary fervently helped campaign for her husband.

145

The Clintons put all their energy into the election campaign. Whenever Bill got discouraged, Hillary encouraged and supported him.

In the end, her self-sacrificing efforts helped her husband get re-elected.

Clinton! Clinton!

Thank you, honey! I couldn't have done it without you.

How about if you keep helping me? How about heading up the education reform that I campaigned about?

Alright. I can handle that.

The public education standards of Arkansas were significantly lower than that of the rest of the country. In order to improve the situation, Clinton identified the main problems and came up with a detailed plan for reform.

I think the state government needs to take full responsibility for improving the students' scores.

We'll conduct an achievement test in every school…

and if more than 15% of a school's students fail the test, we'll have that school participate in a state improvement project.

That's a good idea.

Also, we need to decrease the class size of elementary schools.

And raise the age for compulsory education to 17.

Another thing is to test the teachers.

I knew I asked the right person to take this job! Ha ha ha!

Clinton went around the state speaking about the education reform bill.

This education reform was set in place, and as a result, the standards of the public schools improved greatly.

Arkansas' education reform is doing exceptionally well.

For this and other activities she was involved in, the Arkansas branch of the National Association of Social Workers honored her with the "Best Citizen Award."

All of the reform bills were initiated by Hillary Clinton.

I see. That's quite impressive.

Clinton was named "Arkansas Woman of the Year" by a local newspaper, *the Arkansas Democrat-Gazette.*

In 1991, she was also selected as one of America's 100 most influential lawyers.

Great job, Hillary!

Thanks.

I thought of another plan.

What is it?

It's about a home education program for children before they start school.

In lower-income homes, there are many children who don't go to school. I've been thinking about the necessity of educating children in these circumstances.

I hope this plan can be reflected in an actual policy.

Your ideas and concern for poor children and education just keep coming. I'll see that this gets implemented somehow.

08 Presidential Aspirations

 CD2 Track 29 ▶

After serving as governor of Arkansas for several more terms, Bill Clinton was elected as the 42nd President of the United States on November 3, 1992.

Once again, Hillary had a big part in helping her husband get elected. Clinton quit working at Rose Law Firm and took on her new role as First Lady.

The American health insurance industry and health care system are weak.

Can I do a good job?

The problem is how to drastically lower health costs.

We need to combine the help of the government's management skills and the market's competition.

Yes.

Large companies should cover 80% of their employees' health insurance costs.

The government will cover the total cost of health insurance for the umemployed poor.

This will be the main content for the bill.

If we push our agenda too strongly, the minority party might put up a lot of resistance.

We also have to consider the Congress' ability to revise the bill.

Leave that to me.

Alright.

Although there was a lot of criticism, Hillary Clinton didn't allow any kind of compromise on the health care reform or any of her other plans.

The costs of our proposed system are lower than the existing system, but they're trying to nitpick at anything they can.

We've completed the health care reform bill.

Good job. We'll see what happens when the bill gets presented to Congress.

We'll see what happens.

Clinton presented the bill herself in front of Congress in order to help it get passed.

I learned many things in the last few months while pushing this bill for the American people's health care reform.

I stand here as a mother, a wife, a daughter, a sister, and as an American citizen, and confidently present you with this health care reform bill. I ask you for your careful and wise consideration.

The content of this bill looks pretty good.

I'm surprised we can change so much of the system at such a low cost.

What if this bill actually passes?

Don't worry!

We've been able to knock down every attempt at health care reform so far.

You're right! The physicians' association will be pleased. Hehehe!

Despite the positive response from many congressmen, the health care reform bill that contained Clinton's grand vision didn't pass because of the conservative votes.

How could the bill not pass?

Nobody is on my side. I feel so alone. This is too much to bear!

Sob, sob…

I'm going to make the health care reform happen one way or another.

After the bill got rejected,
Clinton took a diplomatic trip on her own in 1995.
For the first time unaccompanied by
the President, she went with her daughter,
Chelsea for an extended trip abroad.

She traveled through five countries
in Southern Asia, including Pakistan,
India, and Sri Lanka.

The situation for women here is quite hopeless.

But the condition for women around the world has improved incredibly.

The day your own struggles will disappear is not far away.

Thank you.

157

Nearly 1,000 women gathered that day to see her.

Who are all these women?

They're women from all the different villages who wanted to see you.

Mrs. Clinton, I've always wanted to meet you!

Your voice is very hoarse.

I walked for ten hours in the hot sun and dusty air to come here.

No need to do that. Those women are part of the lowest caste, *the untouchables.

What does that mean?

It's best not to make physical contact with them.

Why in the world not? Each one of them is a woman just like me.

She is truly kind. Sob…

It's been a while since I've seen a leader who truly values women.

*The untouchables: the lowest social level of people in India's caste system who are outcasts of society.

I'm Ela Bhatt, the founder of the Self-Employed Women's Association.

You're doing a wonderful work.

Because of you, these women are regaining their self-confidence and…

finding the strength to live in strong solidarity.

I'm just working with the women in India's remote villages. But you are a hope and a light to women all around the world.

You are too kind, Mrs. Bhatt.

Track 35 ▶

Thank you, Mrs. Clinton!

We shall overcome! We will go through hardship and adversity and, in the end, achieve victory!

Too many women, in too many countries, speak the same language, of silence.

It's not just their own suffering they're trying to overcome, but hundreds of years of oppression. Their struggle is truly noble.

These women in the world need to be recognized! If they don't lose hope, the day will come when they will overcome their hardships and we'll all be able to celebrate together!

162

Several months later, the United Nations Fourth World Conference on Women was held in Beijing, China. Clinton participated as the honorary chair of the U.S. delegation.

It's your turn to speak, Mrs. Clinton.

Yes, thank you.

My dear delegates! This is truly a celebration.

A celebration of the contributions women make in every aspect of life: as mothers, wives, sisters, workers, and leaders.

I believe that on the eve of a new millennium, it is time to break our silence. It is no longer acceptable to discuss women's rights as separate from human rights.

The voices of this conference must be heard loud and clear. It is a violation of human rights when babies are denied food or drowned simply because they are born girls.

It is a violation of human rights when women are doused with gasoline, set on fire and burned to death because their marriage dowries are deemed too small.

It is a violation of human rights when a leading cause of death worldwide among women ages fourteen to forty-four is the violence they are subjected to in their own homes by their own relatives.

After returning from a successful time at the U.N. World Conference on Women, Clinton wrote a book on children's issues.

And then in 1998, Hillary Clinton faces a terrible situation she never could have imagined.

Do you have any proof that the Lewinsky scandal was a story created by your political opponents?

This news originated from two lawyers who have been working in the conservative camp.

Clinton confronted this situation with a calm confidence.

That's all for now.

Many people observed how Clinton didn't cower in the worst of situations and instead confronted it with dignity.

That's pretty amazing that she can be so calm through that kind of scandal.

The Time magazine poll that shows Hillary Clinton with a 70% approval rating, for two weeks in a row, says it all.

Clinton demonstrated complete faith in her husband to the end. But after this situation, she began to set out on her own path.

I'm going to run for Senator of New York.

On November 7, 2000, she was elected the Senator of New York.

Hillary!

Hillary!

As Senator, Clinton boosted the economy of upstate New York and committed herself to restoring the environment.

But when *9/11 happened, the state of New York was in utter shock and chaos.

Clinton worked for 70 hours straight during the week after 9/11 to help with the disaster relief.

She requested for $21.5 billion in aid from the federal government.

She also requested the Environmental Protection Agency to test the air quality in the city after 9/11.

Clinton made a smooth transition from being First Lady to Senator, and stepped up to her new role with flying colors.

Right now, helping New York recover and restore normalcy after 9/11 is the most important thing to me. This is my first priority.

While helping to heal the scars of 9/11 on the one hand, Clinton was also busy promoting women's rights in all parts of society.

Clinton resolved to always stand by and act on behalf of fellow American citizens.

And then on January 20, 2007, she officially announced that she would be running to become the Democratic presidential candidate.

All these years, you've given me so much. Now it's my turn to support and help you.

However, Hillary Clinton had a difficult battle to fight with the arrival of a strong opponent named Barack Obama.

Even though your approval ratings are going down, how do you stay so strong?

......

Clinton, who had been running strong in the race, welled up with tears when asked this question.

It is definitely not easy.

Hillary!

In the end, Clinton conceded her defeat to Obama after completing six months of campaigning.

Although she failed to become the Democratic presidential candidate, her excellent abilities were recognized and she was appointed Secretary of State. She is now fully engaged in her work as a global leader.

Her courage, diplomacy, and tolerance are an example to many women around the world.

I want to be like Hillary.

I'm going to be a great politician like her!

Hillary Rodham Clinton is known for her ability to speak
vividly from her experience, interacting with and listening
to people from all walks of life.
Her life, full of determination, vision, and energy,
is one that will be remembered by women
all over the world for years to come.

Word Search

● Find the words which are hidden horizontally, vertically and diagonally.

```
C M Z G A D M I N I S T R A T I O N M R
W O C I E N N I S T N H W W N A H C N I
E B M J A B Q A E T E A R B A R I O B G
R V F M R D C K T V K R R B C D M V H
E C U O E S E N T I H L T T R D E I C T
C X L Q Y N Z O Y X O Q Y Y O E T O X E
O Z F W U D C W C Z G N R U A V E N Z O
N N I E I A E E I A E P W I D R R E A U
T S L R C S G C M S L H H I S G M R S S
R D L U P O H T O E I Y O P D H I B D O
I F R Y H F E Y A T N S V A F E N I F R
B G S U S T I D C R A T E I N G A T G I
U H S I D H M I M H L C R D H O T Y H A
T J A B S O R R F J T I F F J T I F J N
E K N P R O O O R M I A N A T E O G K I
H L A W K F A R D E Y N H H L E N H L B
J Q T M E Q T A U T C O R I T Y M J B L
L W E R L W Y Q L W Y Q L L W Y Q L U E
Z W R E V E C O N F R O N T S U F T J R
X E M E X M R I N C P O E T U R E X N M
W R E M O V E C P R O P H T R Q C I R P
```

commencement	administration	contribute	righteous
nationwide	determination	reform	confront

Vocabulary

• Match each word to the correct meaning.

1. politician   • 기회

2. opportunity   • 상원의원

3. prejudice   • 정치가

4. aspiration   • 국무장관

5. devotion   • 편견

6. senator   • 기량

7. Secretary of State • 변호사

8. governor   • 주지사

9. competence   • 역량

10. tolerance   • 포부

11. prowess   • 헌신

12. attorney   • 인내

Lesson 3 Guess What?

• Guess what she said in the blank.

Lesson 4

Letter to NASA

● Once Hillary Clinton wrote a letter to NASA to be an astronaut. Even though she was rejected, it was an active action to get closer to her dream. Now write your own letter to NASA about why you want to be an astronaut.

Dear NASA,

U.S. Government

Three Branches of U.S. Government

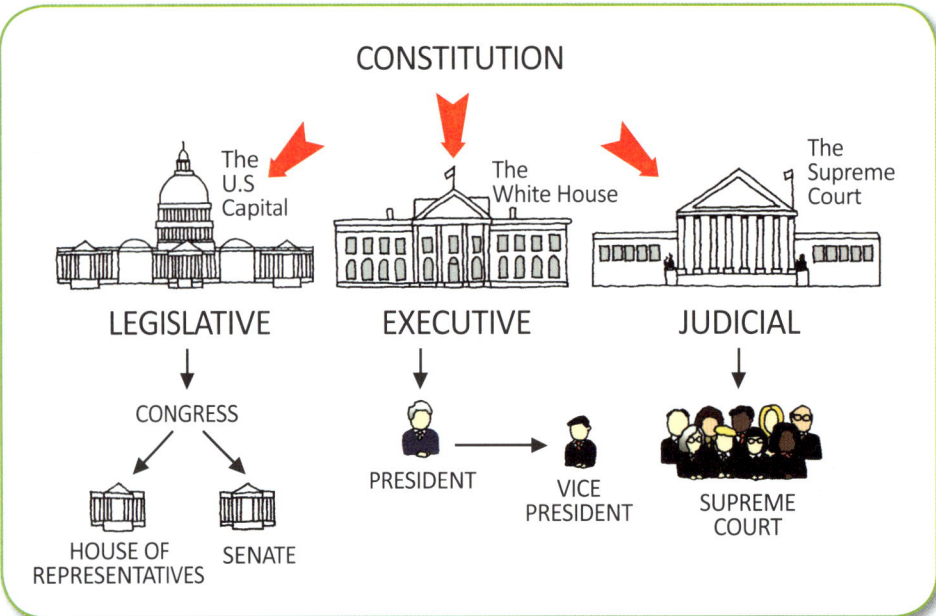

The government runs the country. The democratic government is made up of three parts called legislative(입법부), executive(행정부), judical(사법부) branches. Each branch has its own job to do and makes sure that the other branches don't have too much power.

• The Legislative Branch

 The legislative branch of the U.S. government, or Congress(국회) is made of two groups of people. One group is the Senate(상원) and the other group is the House of Representatives(하원). Their job is to make the laws.

 The Senate has 100 members, two from each state. Senators(상원의원) are elected every 6 years. Hillary Clinton became New York's first female senator.

The House of Representatives is made up of 435 members. A state that has a big population will have more representatives than a state that has a small population. A representative is elected for a term of two years.

Washington D.C(미국의 수도) has no senators or representatives, since it is not a state.

• The Executive Branch

The President(대통령) of the United States is the head of the executive branch of the U.S. government. The President makes sure the laws are carried out and that new laws are made. The President gets help from the Vice President(부통령), and other experts and advisers in certain areas called his cabinet(각료). The President appoints the Cabinet members. The President is the chief commander of the army. The President lives and works in the White House(백악관). The President is elected by the people.

• The Judicial Branch

The Judical branch of government is made up of the court system(법원), and The Supreme Court(대법원) is the highest court. The job of the Supreme Court is to make sure the laws of the country are followed and to settle questions about the laws. Once the Supreme Court makes a decision, it can only be changed by another Supreme Court decision or by amending the Constitution(헌법). The U.S. Supreme Court is made up of nine Justices(대법관). The President appoints justices for the Supreme Court and the Senate approves them. Justices have their jobs for life and works in the Supreme Court Building.

연표

1947년   10월 26일, 시카고에서 아버지 휴 로댐과 어머니 도로시 하웰 로댐 사이에 태어났습니다.

1965년 18세   웰즐리 여자 대학교 입학, 정치학을 전공합니다.

1968년 21세   흑인 민권 운동 지도자 마틴 루터 킹 목사가 암살당합니다. 힐러리가 어린 시절 겪었던 가장 큰 충격적인 사건이었습니다.

1969년 22세   웰즐리 여자 대학교 졸업식에서 학생 최초로 졸업식 연설을 합니다. 같은 해 가을 예일 대학교 법학대학원에 입학합니다.

1970년 23세   빌 클린턴과 만납니다.

1974년 27세   아칸소 대학에서 강의를 시작합니다.

1975년 28세   빌 클린턴과 결혼합니다.

1979년 32세   로즈 법률 사무소 변호사 일을 시작합니다.

1980년 33세   딸 첼시가 태어납니다. 빌 클린턴 아칸소 주지사 연임 실패합니다.

1982년 35세   힐러리 로댐에서 힐러리 클린턴으로 성을 바꿉니다. 클린턴이 주지사에 재당선됩니다.

1992년 45세   모교 웰즐리 여자 대학교 졸업식 연설을 합니다.

1993년 46세   빌 클린턴이 미국 제42대 대통령에 당선됩니다. 힐러리 클린턴은 의료 개혁 책임자에 임명되어 의료 개혁안을 마련하지만 국회에서 통과되지 못합니다.

1995년 48세 『한 명의 아이를 기르려면 온 마을이 합심해야 한다 – 아이들이 우리에게
         알려주는 교훈』을 출간합니다.

2000년 53세 뉴욕 주 상원 의원 경선 출마를 선언하고 공화당 후보 릭 라지오를
         꺾으며 뉴욕 주 상원 의원에 당선됩니다.
         선거에서 공직을 얻은 최초의 영부인으로 기록됩니다.

2003년 56세 자서전 『살아 있는 역사』을 출간합니다.
         2004년 대선 불출마를 선언합니다.
         『뉴스위크』지의 설문 조사 결과 민주당 내에서 가장 이상적인 대통령
         후보 1위에 선정됩니다.

2004년 57세 『타임』지가 주최한 '가장 영향력 있는 100인'에 선정됩니다.

2005년 58세 뉴욕의 여권 단체 국제 여성 건강 연합 선정 '올해의 상'을 수상합니다.
         MSN 엔카르타 주최 '2005년 미국에서 가장 영향력 있는 여성 10인'에
         선정됩니다.

2006년 59세 뉴욕 주 상원 의원에 재당선됩니다.

2007년 60세 2008년 대통령 민주당 후보로 출마할 것을 공식 선언하고 민주당 주최
         2008년 대선 후보 선출을 위한 첫 공식 토론회 참여합니다.

2008년 61세 민주당 내 대선 후보를 가리는 아이오와 주에서 열린 첫 당원 대회에서
         오바마에게 패합니다. 뉴햄프셔 예비 선거에서는 힐러리가 승리합니다.

2009년 62세 미국 국무장관에 임명됩니다.

Biography Comic who?

who? 01	Barack Obama	979-11-5639-023-7
who? 02	Charles Darwin	979-11-5639-024-4
who? 03	Bill Gates	979-11-5639-025-1
who? 04	Hillary Clinton	979-11-5639-026-8
who? 05	Stephen Hawking	979-11-5639-027-5
who? 06	Oprah Winfrey	979-11-5639-028-2
who? 07	Steven Spielberg	979-11-5639-029-9
who? 08	Thomas Edison	979-11-5639-030-5
who? 09	Abraham Lincoln	979-11-5639-031-2
who? 10	Martin Luther King, Jr.	979-11-5639-032-9
who? 11	Louis Braille	979-11-5639-033-6
who? 12	Albert Einstein	979-11-5639-034-3
who? 13	Jane Goodall	979-11-5639-035-0
who? 14	Walt Disney	979-11-5639-036-7
who? 15	Winston Churchill	979-11-5639-037-4
who? 16	Warren Buffett	979-11-5639-008-4
who? 17	Nelson Mandela	979-11-5639-009-1
who? 18	Steve Jobs	979-11-5639-010-7
who? 19	J. K. Rowling	979-11-5639-011-4
who? 20	Jean-Henri Fabre	979-11-5639-012-1
who? 21	Vincent van Gogh	979-11-5639-013-8
who? 22	Marie Curie	979-11-5639-014-5
who? 23	Henry David Thoreau	979-11-5639-015-2
who? 24	Andrew Carnegie	979-11-5639-016-9
who? 25	Coco Chanel	979-11-5639-017-6
who? 26	Charlie Chaplin	979-11-5639-018-3
who? 27	Ho Chi Minh	979-11-5639-019-0
who? 28	Ludwig van Beethoven	979-11-5639-020-6
who? 29	Mao Zedong	979-11-5639-021-3
who? 30	Kim Dae-jung	979-11-5639-022-0